■ Fruit

■ Fruit

■ Vegetables

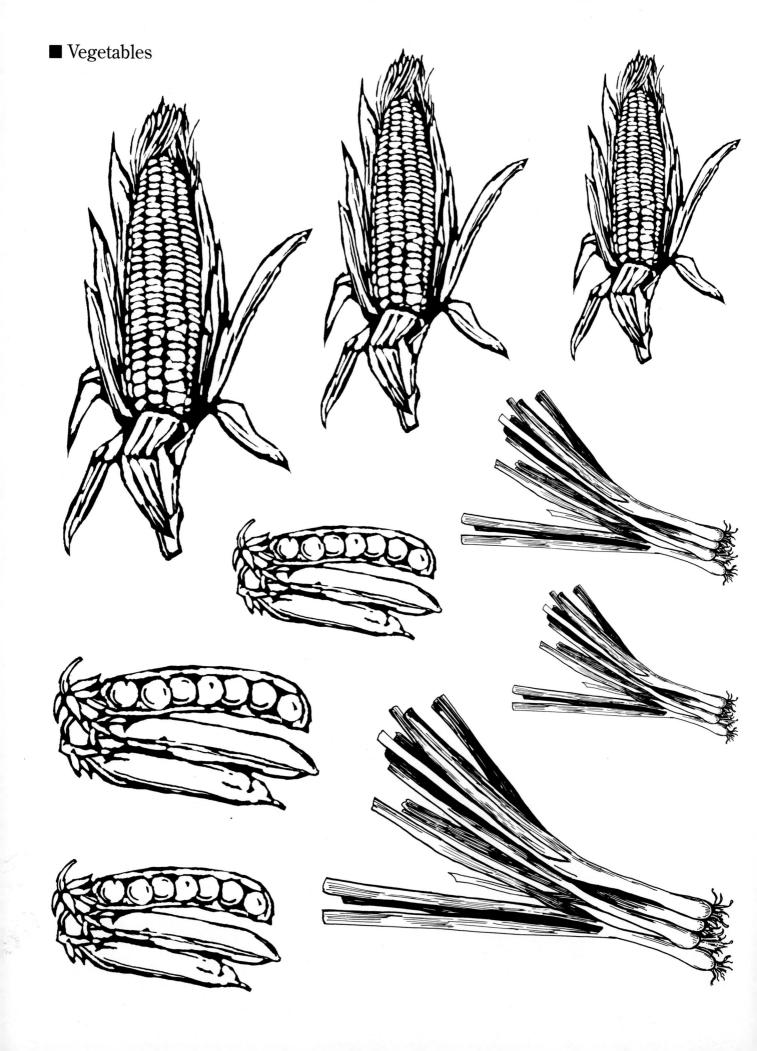

■ Vegetables

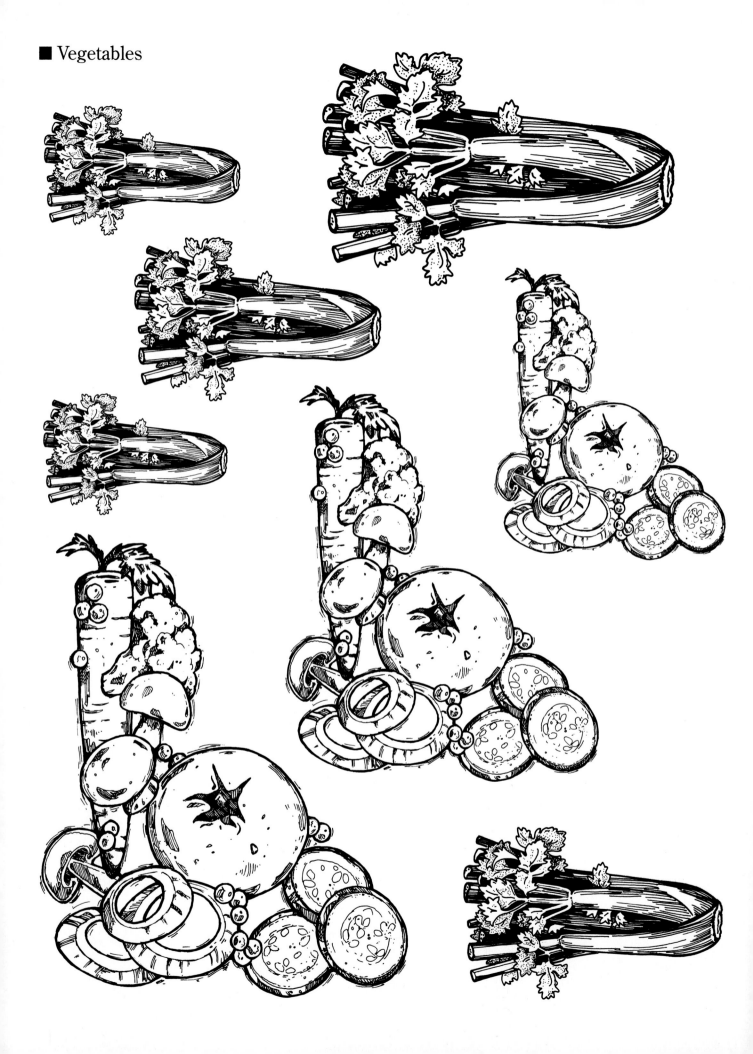

■ Vegetables

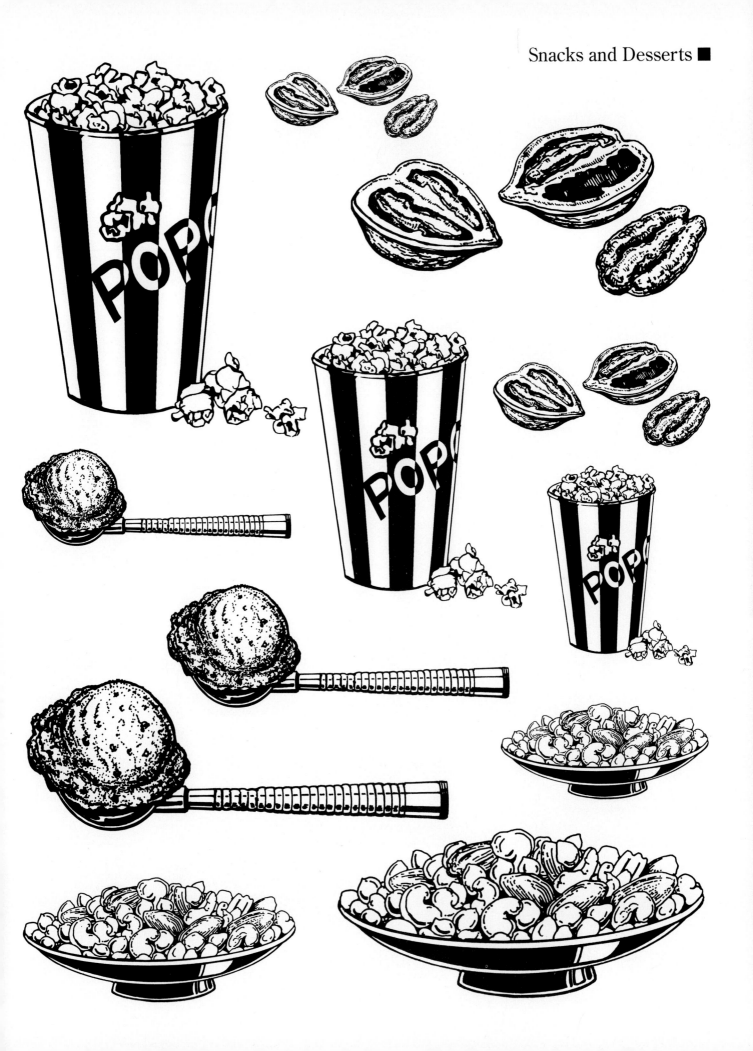

The Food Pyramid

■ Fish, Fowl and Meat

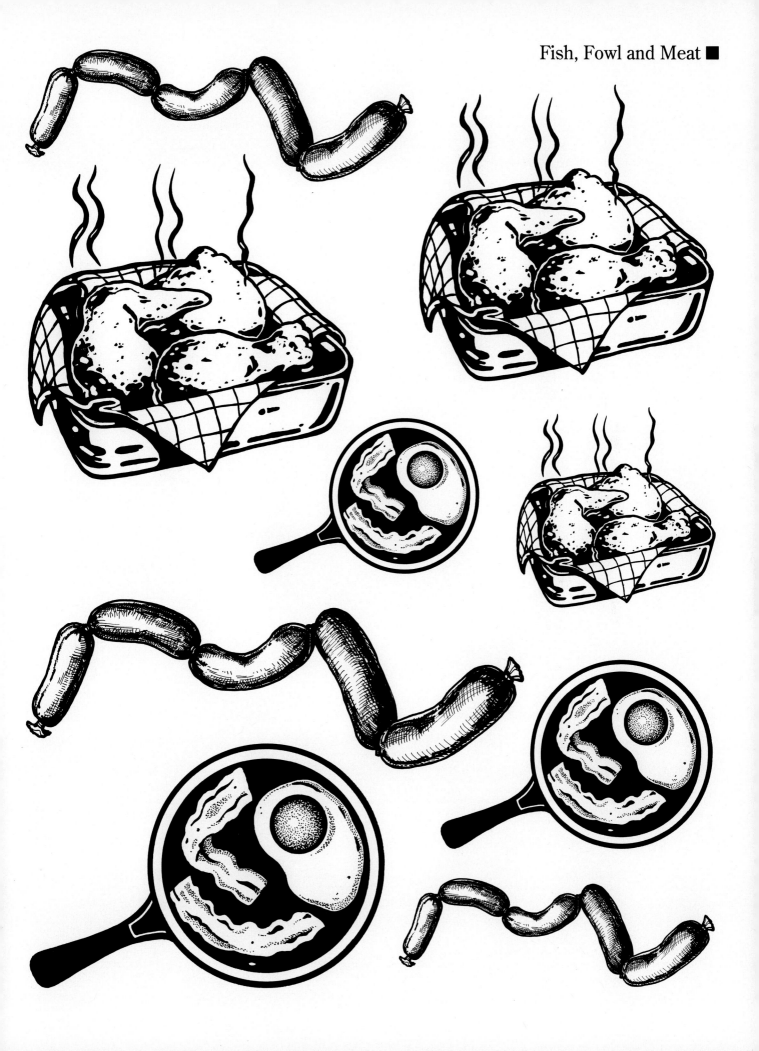

■ Fish, Fowl and Meat

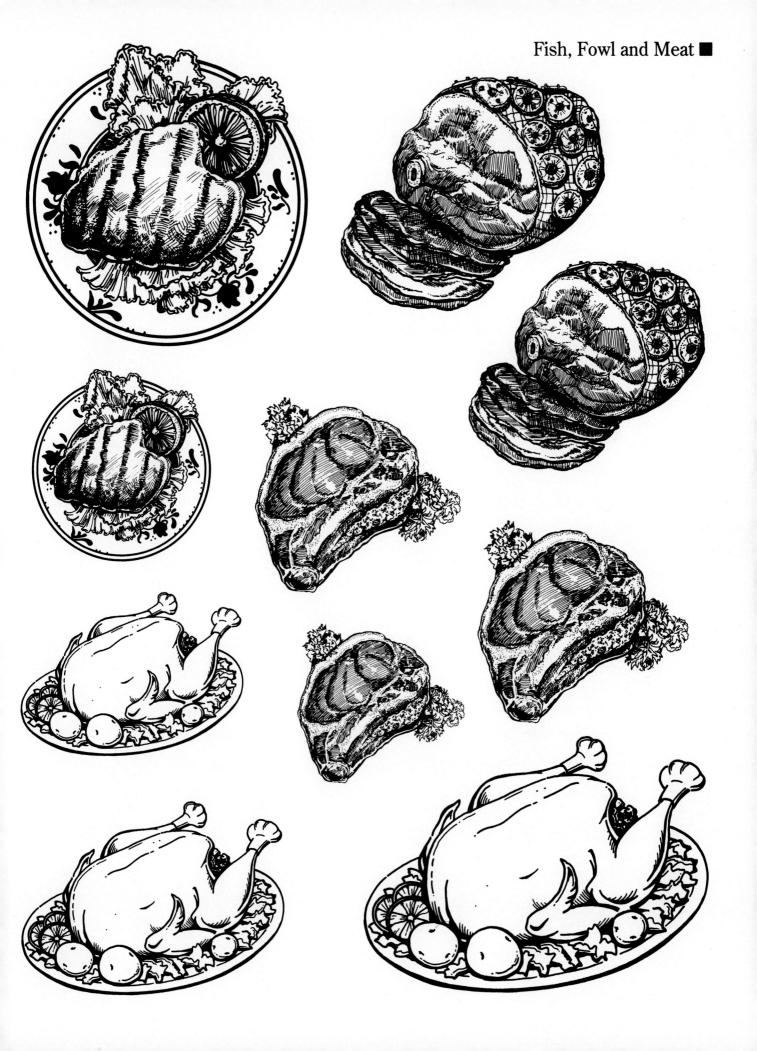

■ Fish, Fowl and Meat

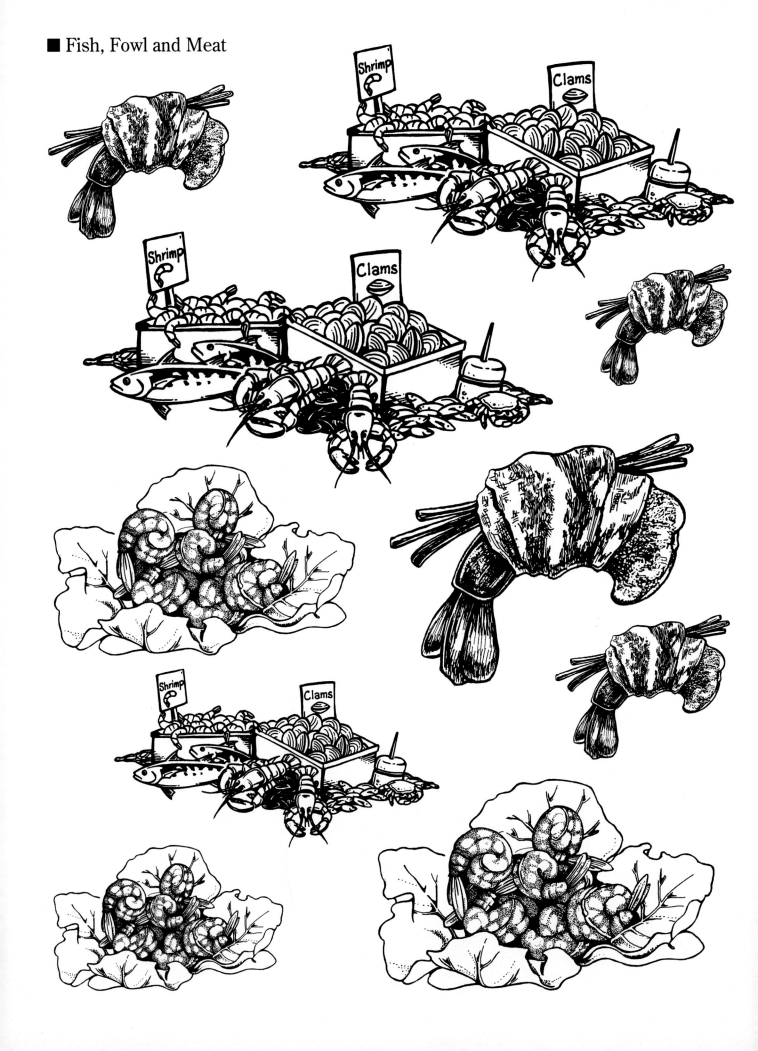

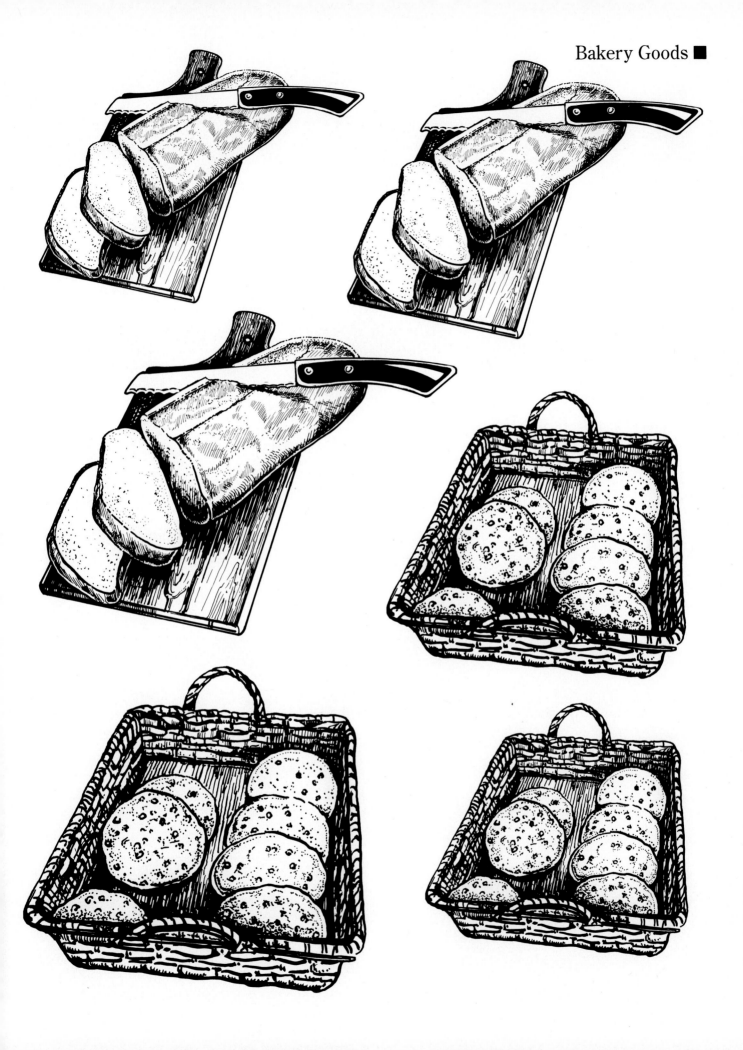

■ Bakery Goods

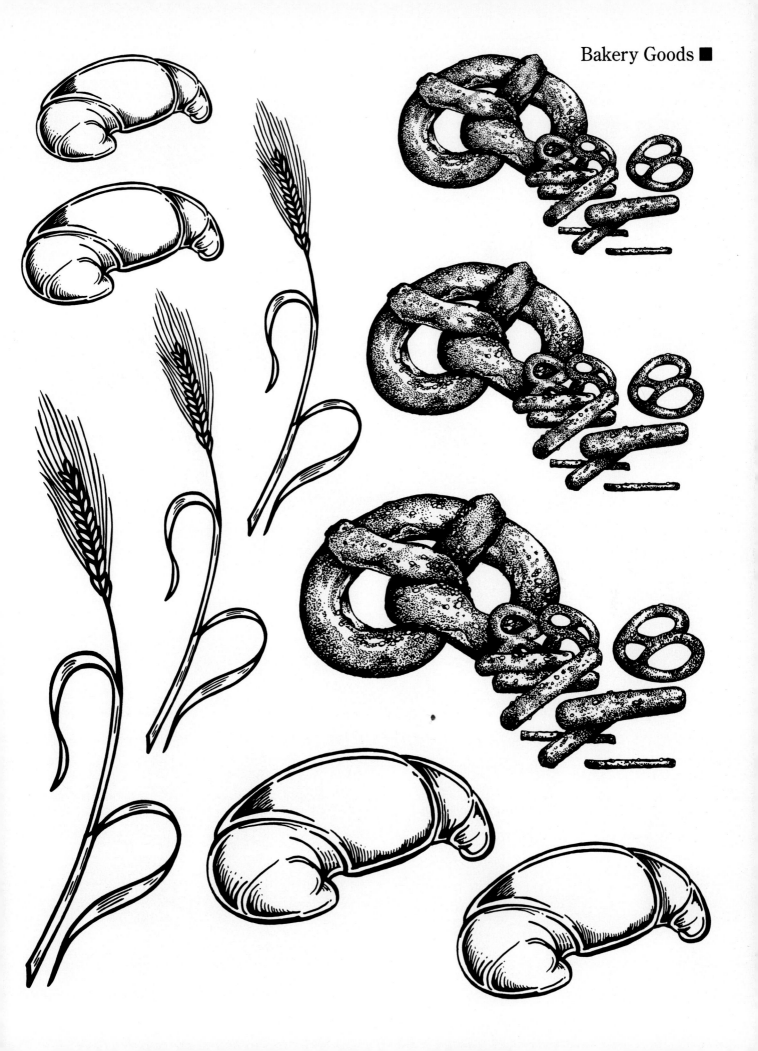

■ Food Specialties

■ Food Specialties